THE INTENTIONAL WOMAN

A timeless guide for the multi-faceted, multi-gifted, purpose-filled woman

BY

Kamisha Young

Table of Contents

Introduction: You have what it takes

To the woman reading this, you've got it. Let's start there. What is "it"? Well, I'm glad you asked. You have what it takes to become an intentional woman of excellence. You were created with intention by God. He had a purpose and a plan for you when you were created, fashioned, and in your mother's womb. This is the first fact we need to establish. You are here for a reason, and God has a plan for you from the beginning to the end. The reason we have to accept this fact early on is because it's shaping our lives as we speak. The way you walk, talk, and interact with others, the way you handle conflicts, the way you think about yourself and everyone around you has everything to do with your beliefs about yourself. Do you believe that you're just here out of pure "luck and chance"? Do you think it's just a matter of time before life will deal you a bad hand like everyone else you see on the news, in the media, or on your phone? Or do you truly believe that you have a great purpose on this earth every day when you wake up with breath in your body? My sincere hope for you as you read this is that you are reminded of your value, you are re-ignited in your purpose, and you begin to go forward with the plans of God for your life. God's plan for you never stops, slows down or gets thrown away due to life events, losses, or setbacks. It's up to us to navigate and continue forward each day. That's what this guide is for: to equip you with the wisdom and knowledge that you need to continue in your journey. Knowledge is power, and wisdom is more valuable than gold. If you have those two things, you lady will become unstoppable. No storm, no trial or test, or even heartbreak will be able to stop you. You will be so intentional that you will go through life with clarity, confidence, and excellence. You will have strategy and solutions, grace and grit, peace and power. You will be the woman who creates change for the better and does it with excellence. You have what it takes. Now, let's get to it.

Chapter 1

Look no farther, look within

Many have heard the term "comparison is the thief of joy," and I believe this is accurate in so many ways. For you to operate as an intentional woman, you need to fix your focus in the right position. You need to take your focus off of anything and anyone that is not helping you become the woman you desire to be. You certainly want to take your eyes off of others. Hear me; you've got work to do. You've got a treasure inside of you that needs to be unlocked. You are filled with gifts, talents, and abilities. You have a responsibility for the season that you are in right now. Doesn't matter how "unglamorous" it makes you look or feel at the moment. You might be thinking, "What's so great about where I am right now?" But I'm here to tell you that there's a great assignment before you right now. Sometimes, we are too distorted and distracted by the cares of this world, events, tragedies, and external factors, and we lose sight of our main purpose each day. That purpose is to wake up in the morning, go out and operate in the calling of God for our lives. For some, a daily calling can be a single woman devoting her life to living as God's daughter, allowing her light to shine at school, on her job, in her family, and wherever her feet may go, for another, her assignment may be a wife and mother, a maker of her home, stewarding the upbringing of her children, caring for her husband and making sure she is helping him with the vision of the family, or even a single mother who's main assignment in this season is loving herself and her children, providing for her house and learning how to lead and depend on God to supply her protection, needs, and direction. There are so many roles that we as women have, and I want to emphasize that no one's role is more significant than another's. The grass is not greener on anyone else's lawn. If it begins to look that way, it's only because you're neglecting your garden. You've got to look within. You've got to look inside and see what God has graced and blessed you with, then really aim to see the value in it. Has God blessed you with children? Then, you need to be an intentional mother who takes hold of the role of a mother with joy and wisdom. The call of a mother is filled with many different dimensions, and that in itself is reason enough to look inside and make sure that what's inside of you is something that you are eager and happy about duplicating with your children. What is in you comes out of you. Everyone in your life is feeding off what you carry. Looking within means that you are open to seeing the truth about yourself, ready to be self-aware, and ready to make the necessary adjustments to become that intentional woman. You can never make that transition if you are stuck focusing on the next woman, what season of her life she's in, why you haven't entered yours yet, why you can't seem to have it "all together" like her and so forth and so on. Those things are distractions, time wasters, and joy killers, but we will talk a bit more about them later. The bottom line is this journey is all about you. It's not about anyone else. Everyone that you are connected to, assigned to and live life with needs you. They need you to spend the time searching on the inside. They need you to pause and focus on yourself. Why? Because you directly impact the people in your life. The conversations that you carry directly impact someone else; the way you do your job impacts another; the way you love your spouse, your children, and your family

5

impacts another generation of your bloodline. It's not enough to say, "This is my life, and I can do what I want." no sis. Your life is not just yours; it was given to you by God, bought at a price, and you have a responsibility to live it out with care and intention. You are not just a no-name "Jane" of the world. You are a child of God who was born for a reason. Once you start believing and knowing you are, you'll begin to move. Differently, you'll begin to see yourself in the right lens. You'll know that you carry power and purpose on the inside of you, yet you'll remain humble in understanding that it was given to you by God, so no, you're not exactly "self-made" because you didn't create yourself. You may feel like you took part in creating a beautiful, thriving family or that you built that business from the ground up; maybe you are getting an education and accreditation that reflects your determination and hard work. That's great and something to be thankful for. Yet, it's God's goodness, grace, and unwavering mercy that God brought you this far. Therefore, as you read and digest the rest of this book, I want you to see it from that perspective. You cannot be passive about your life because God is not passive about you. He was not passive about the times he protected you from danger, the times he covered you from things you don't even know about, the times he heard you when you cried out to him. We hear the phrase, "God doesn't play about me." People say this when they affirm the goodness of God, and he shows himself in their lives. I've used the phrase myself before because I truly do believe that about my life. I've seen God do things for me that no one else could do, I've seen him open doors no one else could open, and I've also seen God take the lowest times of my life and use them for my greater good. At the same time, as I believe God doesn't play about me, I don't take lightly my life and living for him. I don't go around living on a whim, doing what I want, saying and acting in any way, letting my feelings and emotions rule me, and following after my wants by acknowledging God. Why? Because I want to be worthy of the life he gave me. I want to show him on a daily basis that I appreciate his love and kindness toward me. When I fall short, I want God to know I love him enough to change what he is correcting in me. I aim to humble myself before him so he can continue to protect me, cover me, and favor me. I want that same lifestyle for you. Greater heights and greater levels over your life. If you want to live your life on a higher level than "average", if you want to experience joy that doesn't end with a holiday season, a birthday, or a special event but one that resides inside of you even in your worst days, keep reading. I'm going to share with you divine wisdom and action steps on how to become an intentional

a woman who impacts this world and hears from God at all times.

Chapter 2

She knows what she carries

Living as an intentional woman means that you know exactly what you carry on the inside of you. I'm not talking about how your hair is done, the clothes that you wear, that expensive bag that you toss around and pride yourself on purchasing. I'm literally talking about knowing what's inside of you. Do you know that what is in you no one else can possess? Do you know your worth?

Who are you?

Do you know who you really are on the inside? Do you know your identity that God has given you, understanding this: that God created you with purpose on purpose? The personality that you have is not by mistake, not by chance. Everything you've gone through and everything you've experienced in life has been on purpose to get you where you are today. It's important to understand that in order to navigate through life with intention if you never understand your identity, you will go through life just believing that you're a problem or you're too loud you're too you're too hard to deal with those types of things. I feel like; as women, we oftentimes will deal with those barriers and challenges from other people who project or know based on where they are; listen to me if you understand your identity. You own it; there will not be a person or a situation that can shake your identity and who you are. A woman who knows her identity is confident, secure, and safe in who she is. She is not out to get another woman. She's not putting down another woman in order to lift herself, but she's able to celebrate herself while still crowning the next woman, still celebrating the gifts, talents and value that she sees in her fellow sister. This is why I love being around women who know who they are; I never have to worry about them coming for who I am, trying to knock me down, or trying to undermine the things that are on the inside of me. If you find yourself around these types of people all the time, you may want to ask yourself, what inside of you is attracting these types of people? Sometimes, we mean well, but we don't realize that we are seeking external validation from people who are not even accepting of who we are. This is why it's so important to not only know your identity but also be able to walk boldly and confidently in your identity. Who you are is not everyone's cup of tea. Everyone will not be drawn to you.

As good of a person as you may be, some people will not be for you, and that is OK, but learning who you are on the inside will prevent you many times from wanting to sit at tables where you're not even welcome or wanting to have opportunities with people that aren't even fitting in your future. Knowing my identity as a child of God and understanding the person that I was designed to be have been great blessings and game-changers in the way that I operate in my everyday life. I understand that some things about me may come off a bit too strong for other ladies or other people in general. I get that my determination and my drive in life are not always going to be accepted by those who are content with living a mediocre or bare minimum lifestyle. Sometimes, the simple act of being Kamisha is just too much for some people and guess what? I do not take that personally. I do not take that as something being wrong with me; I don't even take it as something being wrong with that person. We are just two people that do not align. We're not going in the same direction, and we may not speak the same language, but

11

that is OK. On the flip side of it, walking in your true identity, you will be able to draw those people who are for you or who are meant to help you and align with you in your life and your destiny. You will be able to make decisions about that quickly. As intentional women, we are to be able to detect, discern, and decide on a daily basis what is right for us at all times. We are to be able to make sound and sober decisions that will help us for the better. If you don't know who you are at your core, others will tell you who you are, and they will lead you down a path that may not be right for your destiny. They can send you down a cycle of stagnation, limitation, and dysfunction. So, at all costs, focus on understanding your true identity. It will matter in everything that you do.

Girl, you are a gift.

Did you know that you're a gift, a jewel and treasure to be unlocked? How do I know this? I am certain of it because God created you, and anything God creates is a masterpiece. Now, in order for you to operate intentionally, you need to understand that you carry gifts, talents, and abilities that are supposed to be used inside of you. There's something you're good at doing. There's a part of you that comes naturally to you. There is a solution on the inside of you that is meant to solve a problem here on this earth, and I need you to understand that no gift is too small when it's used effectively. Now, could you stick with me? Have you ever been in the kitchen cooking something and needed a can opener? You might say, "How is a can opener such a treasure"? It literally only costs a couple of bucks, and you don't even need it all the time in the kitchen, but guess what? When you need it, it is very necessary. I remember the times when I was younger, trying to cook in the kitchen, and I could not find the can opener. I tried to use an actual knife to open up the can, and I actually managed to get somehow it open, but I risked cutting myself. It took so long that the edges were jagged; it was just a hot mess, and by the time I actually got the can open, I really wasn't in the mood to even be cooking anymore. My point is that your gift is valuable, and it makes things better. It makes a situation easier. It solves a problem, so it does not matter how insignificant you feel that your gift is; it is still valuable at the right time, in the right place, in the right room. Your gift is gold. Protect your gift, protect the talent on the inside of you that God has given you, but don't hide it. The word of God even says that light cannot be hidden under a bushel, but it needs to be put on its stand so that it gives light to everyone in the house. (Matt. 5:15). Your gift matters. You need to know how to use it effectively. I'm not telling you to go out and scream on the mountaintop that you're the greatest singer or that you're the best cook or that you have the greatest gift of prophecy in the world, but what I'm telling you is know what you carry. Know the proper time to use your gift and know the time to remain hidden and protect what you have.

She's diligent and consistent.

It's not just enough to know what you carry; you also have to be diligent and consistent with what's on your inside. That is going to be the difference maker in the success of being an intentional woman. Every day is not going to feel like sunshine and rainbows, but when you have diligence and consistency in your life, it will always speak for itself. Let's say you have a goal to start living out a healthy lifestyle, focusing on your wellness, taking care of your body, and focusing on your spiritual and mental health. You want to be consistent in this. You don't want to be up one day, down the next, be calm one minute, or tell somebody off the next minute. You want to be diligent and consistent in this lifestyle that you are creating. This will cause others to look at you and say, " I know exactly what she stands for; I know what she's made of. I know what I can expect from her." That is what being an intentional woman will produce. It will make your actions speak for themselves, and you will not have to bust down any doors or opportunities when you are diligent and consistent.

When you go to the gym, you eat healthy, and you commit to a healthy lifestyle, and it will show up on you. You will look like you took time to focus on your health and your wellness. When you take care of your finances and set those goals, the products of productivity and abundance will speak for themselves. People will start to ask you, "How did you do that? How are you managing what you do with the job that you work? How are you managing this business that you're running?" It causes other people to seek you out instead of you begging someone else to sit at their table and be a part of what they have going on, and you will begin to get invitations. People will want you to be a part of contributing to what they have. You might be called on to be a solution to a problem that they are seeking out, so you never have to tote your own horn. You don't have to go out of your way to cut down anyone else, but your consistency and your diligence will always speak louder than your words.

She's self-aware and open to improvement.

An intentional woman is always making adjustments in her life because she realizes that there's power in ongoing growth, change and elevation. Now, in this process, we must also learn to be content with where we are. So this is not to say that we're running a rat race to get to the next level, but we also are not shrinking in order to be comfortable and avoid growth. No, we are taking the opportunities as they come. There have been so many times in my life when I've done self-reflection, and I realize that I have room to grow in certain areas; the opportunities are endless when you open up your mind to that possibility. Being open to growth makes you a teachable woman, and a teachable woman becomes a powerful woman. There are times when you are not always the expert in your field. You are not always the go-to person. There are times when you have to be a student, and this is the opportunity to listen, observe, process and learn. Then, at the right time, You will be able to walk into that as

16

an expert or a leader, but it's OK when there are times that you may not always be the leader but a novice. This is why it's important to get in rooms where you are not always at the top, where you are the one that needs to be learning. You are the one that needs to be poured into, and you're the one that needs to be taught. This also keeps us walking in humility because it's so easy to receive when we know that we're also a student and a teacher. This keeps us from feeling inadequate during times when we should be receptive to another person, giving us the proper feedback or constructive criticism to help us to the next level without us going down a negative hole of self-loathing, resentment, and resistance.

Don't resist the opportunity to grow. Don't avoid that tough conversation that you may need to have with a friend when she's telling you that you can be doing better or she's asking you about those goals that you shared with her at the beginning of the year. Don't fight the urge to expand. An intentional woman is a receptive and receiving woman. She understands that this is a part of her process of becoming the very best version of herself.

Chapter 3

She walks with grace and power

Agraceful woman can accomplish many things. She knows that being a woman in her fullest capacity is not a sign of weakness or a shortcoming. It's who God designed her to be and how he intended for her to operate. Being a graceful woman means knowing how to handle yourself in situations. Being able to empathize and understand others that may be different from you. Having compassion and a nurturing heart that can trust, give, and receive. A graceful woman is healed and whole. She isn't defensive and doesn't have a tough exterior or a calloused heart, but she is soft, agile, and elegant in how she handles life and the world around her. When you walk into the room, how is your presence perceived as a woman? Do people turn away due to the look on your face, the way you may walk in the room, or how you address others? Are people drawn to you? Do people want to interact with you because of your countenance, your openness, the smile or the expression on your face? I've met plenty of very nice women who say they are kind-hearted but have a mean resting face. While we shouldn't judge a book by its cover, the truth is this is how people will create their first impression of you many times. When you walk into a place to conduct business, people will address you based on your countenance, mannerisms, and appearance. It's just the way of the world. It's the way we make a quick judgment. Sometimes, you will not always have the opportunity to show people who you really are or even have a conversation with them. Your first impression will make or break you.

There were two times in my life when I went to inquire about a job position, and the company was not currently hiring, but I got the job. It was due to my mannerisms, disposition, and first impression. The store owner told me she liked the way I spoke and asked about the job, and she called me a week later about a position. The second occasion was a store employee who asked for my name and email after a quick 5-minute conversation we had. He said I would be great with the type of clientele the store served. I shared these two examples in my life to let you know that grace is a key that grants access. When you become refined as a woman and learn how to carry

20

yourself and have an authenticity to you that is also kind and easy to be around, it will get you places that money alone cannot. Here are some characteristics of a graceful woman:

- Soft
- Sophisticated
- Gentle
- Calm
- Joyful
- Kind
- Respectful
- Courteous
- Considerate
- Confident
- Poised
- Caring
- Refined

These are some characteristics associated with a graceful woman. These traits will make her powerful. What does power mean to you? Impact is the word that comes to mind for me. The ability to positively influence someone and make a difference. When a woman can gain control of herself, properly manage her emotions, and take hold of her spiritual health and growth, then she is able to have the power to impact another person. Sis, why would you want to run a large business with several employees if you cannot hold yourself accountable for the way you work or deal with others? This is why, as intentional women, we should always look to improve ourselves so that others can be positively impactful.

What is power?

1. The ability to do something or act in a particular way, especially as a faculty or quality.

2. The capacity or ability to direct or influence the behavior of others or the course of events.

In both of these formal definitions, the two words that are the same are Ability.

Power is simply the ability to do what needs to be done. It can obtain information, process it, and carry it out in an effective manner. You hold power in your life; however, if you are not aware of it or know how to use your power properly, you will have a limited life. God's holy Spirit gives us power (Acts 1:8). It is not something that is only demonstrated during an assembled service at church; it is an ability that is used throughout our everyday lives. It gives you the power to speak in a room when everyone sees and answers, and you have the solution. It allows you to remain quiet in a time of chaos and know how to bring an atmosphere of calm and peace. It helps you to speak about a topic that is not popular but necessary. It gives you the strength to care for your baby in the late night hours and early mornings because, as a mother, you know they depend on you. Power use effectively is a wonderful tool. Power used ineffectively can be a nightmare.

Your words have the power.

How you choose to use your words can make or break your situation; they can make or break a person. This is why, as an intentional woman, you have to own the fact that your words carry weight. While it is true that words have power, you have to be a good steward of your words, and this starts with how you speak to yourself and about yourself. If you are a woman who is always speaking negatively about yourself, talking down about yourself or even those inner thoughts that you may have that come out, "Oh, I'm so stupid I can't get anything right," "Oh my gosh I don't know why I'm always making dumb decisions." Then let me tell you something: you are being very careless with the power that you have been given for your words. Your words have the power to heal or hurt. Your words could position people to their purpose or poison them with toxicity. Your words can lift. Your words can also tear you down. Your words can bring answers and solutions, or your words can cause chaos and exhaustion to people.

Which woman do you want to be known for? Ask yourself this question, "When I think about myself in the quiet, still moments, how do I really feel about myself right now?" "Do I believe I'm a beautiful woman full of possibility, love and good things? Or do I believe that I'm just here, I don't look good, I never feel good, and I'm just trying to get by day by day?" These inner thoughts or thoughts about yourself have a direct correlation with the thoughts that you think toward others. There's no way that you would ever be able to properly celebrate, appreciate or cultivate the life of another person through your words if you cannot first do the same for yourself. You are your greatest investment. You are your first partaker of the words that you speak, so you need to learn how to align your words with the woman that you believe you are, the woman that you're also becoming. At this current phase of my life, I truly enjoy being around other women who understand their power. This, to me, is such a gift because women who know their power understand how to speak life to themselves and speak life to those around them. I love it when my friend shares something with me that will lift me, hold me accountable, correct me, / or help me become a better version of myself. I never willingly surround myself with people who intentionally want to tear me down or project their low self-esteem or their lack of appreciation of themselves onto me as a person. I want people around me who are not afraid to tell me the truth, love me, and bring out the best in me. As an intentional woman, that is what you should desire as well. You should not have anyone in your life by default. Meaning you allow them a rent-free space in your life, knowing that they do not add, they do not contribute, nor do they help you become a better person. You should not be allowing people in your life who use their words to bring you harm mentally, emotionally, or spiritually. You have to learn that you are worth more than a toxic environment. You're worth more than a toxic relationship, and you're worth more than just having someone in your presence. Sometimes, it's better to be alone than to accept people in your life who are pulling you down from the place that you and God desire for you to be.

Power doesn't have anything to prove

When you operate in true power and not just your ego, you realize you don't have anything to prove. This is learning how to properly steward your power, knowing that there's a time for you to speak up, be assertive, take authority make things happen, but then there's also a time to use your power to remain silent, to turn a deaf ear to things that are said to put a trap in your life, to remain quiet in a compromising situation, where people want to gossip and slander or say things that are not true, this type of power goes along with having emotional intelligence emotional control, and wisdom. The Bible also refers to this as temperance, another fruit of the spirit. Hear what I'm saying: being intentional does not mean that you will not face conflicts, difficulties or challenges, but it does mean that you will know how to handle these moments with poise, grace, and tact. Power gives you the ability to forgive a person that you know has wronged you, but instead, you pardon the wrongdoing, restore it and move forward. Power gives you the ability to hold your peace in a moment where you could say so many valid things that would hurt a person who aimed to hurt you, but instead of trying to even the score and get a lick back, you choose to show them grace and put a smile on and continue with your assignment of life. I learned my power as a woman even more when I got married to my husband, and we've been married for a few years.

I finally learned that the best way to get through to my husband, to understand my point of view in a situation, was not to nag him and try to control the way he thought but to love him, serve him and be his friend. Then, at the right time, I will be able to make my request known, speak my differences, and position myself in a way that my words will be received. I also learned in being married and married how less words hold more weight. I really learned the impact of my words when it comes to my husband, knowing that he takes what I say. He really does take an account of how I feel. Still, there were times in the past when my words were so diluted because I spent so much time just talking, nagging, over-explaining, and repeating a lot of the same things, and instead of him being able to focus on my points, he was focusing on my tone of voice, my delivery or my sense of control behind what I was really trying to say. Now, I can honestly say being happily married to my husband, we have better communication, and we're able to effectively share because I've learned that it doesn't take me repeating the same thing 20 times to him. It may take me saying one thing, one time, in a pleasant way, and he will "get it." There have even been times in my marriage when I learned that silence speaks louder than a lot of words and jargon. This is not to say that you are supposed to give someone the "silent treatment" as a punishment if you're not satisfied in an area. No, I'm not saying that, nor do I condone those types of behaviors that are not healthy. What I am saying is if you've already expressed yourself one time about a situation or circumstance, that person likely knows how you feel. So, the next time it occurs, or the next time you might be faced with it, silence is the best to give that person a chance to remember what you already said, and they are able to process what it is and how they can change the action.

She knows when to listen.

An intentional woman who is filled with grace and power is not always out to make her point or shout from the rooftops about her knowledge, but she's also very well crafted at being a good listener. A good listener is a person who takes the time to understand others, refrains from speaking at times, and really hears the heart and the root of the matter in any situation. A woman who listens well is a woman who gains trust, understanding, and access on a deeper level. We live in a world where we're always consuming information and trying to find out what's going on, but there are very few opportunities for us to listen to what others are saying in order to gain insight into the matters at hand. I know that as women, we automatically create it by using our words to express our feelings and our needs, but one good skill as a woman would be practicing the art of being a great listener. Listening may not be your strong point as a woman because you may just be inclined to speak right after someone says something or to give your opinion at every point that you may hear; however, listening is winning. Listening is also gaining knowledge. Listening is building. Listening is understanding and a form of power.

29

The more you know, the more you're able to assess, help and create an impact properly. If you're a parent, one of the greatest things that you will learn to do is listen to your children. It is your responsibility to teach them, show them, demonstrate, and correct all those things that are highly necessary. Listening is also a key as a mom; you learn to listen to your child's cry from the moment they are born. Many parents learn that certain cries mean certain things. One cry might mean you need to be changed. One cry is different from needing sleep or being sick; it's a sound and an inclined ear that it takes to know how to care for this person. No matter what your capacity is, how much education you have, your expertise, or the business field you may be in, it is always going to help you. Listening to your clients, listening to the Holy Spirit and what he may need to let you know about a situation or if you're in a conversation with a person and you realize they're not necessarily comfortable telling you everything that is going on with him they might be dealing with embarrassment, shame, or guilt or just flat out, able to express themselves to how they're feeling, listen to what their body language is showing you, listen to their tone of voice and be able to help them through properly but they

30

dealing with. This makes you a powerful and intentional woman, knowing how to put a smile on a child's face when you see them afraid or crying. Being able to use what's inside of you to edify or enable someone else. It can go a long way.

Chapter 4

She stewards well and knows her boundaries

A woman who stewards well is a treasure to behold. Stewardship is the careful management of sorting that has been entrusted to one's care. As women, we are to be effective in managing the multiple facets of our lives. The better we become at stewardship, the more we can be trusted with it on a greater level. As a woman of God, we should strive to steward things in our lives with excellence because we serve a great God. He is not a mediocre God who does the bare minimum; God never did anything halfway; he created the earth with great intent and purpose. He created you with great intent and ability on the inside of you. Even your physical body was made intentionally. If you have all fingers and toes, you can see that he is in the details. Look at the hair on your head. Its density, It's color, and shape are not a mistake. When we realize that all parts of our life are a gift, we will become better stewards. What you may be a steward over can vary from one woman to another, but we still have a few things in common. As we move further into this chapter, we will take a look at some of the foundational areas in which we can intentionally be good stewards.

She stewards her time well.

You may heard the saying, "We all have the same 24 hours in a day." I will say it's true. However, during the day, we may have different responsibilities. Does it change the fact that we can all effectively manage our time? I believe we can. In the area of time, we can also see our self-worth, values, and mindsets. Here, some people view time as "I will never have enough time in a day to do what I need to." While others choose to eliminate the excuses and the mental blocks and "Just do it," I'm a person of the latter. I've always had the mindset that I can get it done. Have I always been excellent with my stewardship? Not at all. I had to have years of growth, mistakes, and experience to teach me how to steward better. I've missed deadlines, being late for important occasions, I've missed a few opportunities as a cost of my level of stewardship. Yet, it taught me how to improve. I remember having a conversation with my college professor over 10 years ago.

(I'm telling my age here) but she held me back after a class to give me some hard feedback. We had a class presentation in one of my early childhood education courses, and part of the presentation was peer review. My peers graded me very high, helping my overall presentation score. However, my professor's portion of my presentation was not to my liking. It was more of a "C" score, and my peers graded me on an "A," so my average presentation came out to a B. I was satisfied, honestly. As a 19-year-old, I didn't see an issue with it. I presented very confidently, dressed well, and spoke with intention. However, when my professor spoke to me, she said that she was not satisfied with my work. She said that in reviewing my actual work, she could tell I did not spend the appropriate time and effort on my presentation. She said, "You have a gift of speaking, and you presented in front of the class very well because you're just good at it, but there were others in here who did twice the work you did but didn't present as well as you, so they ended up with a lower grade." She proceeded to say how she knows I am capable of more. She knows that I could have done more research, and She put more effort into the work. Over ten years later, that conversation marked my

34

life. It made me think about the way I stewarded my college work, my projects, and my assignments, which then trickled over into my post-graduate career. When I got hired by companies, I made a point of being a good steward. Even though I could "get it done," I wanted to make sure I did it right and thoroughly. I wanted to have integrity behind my work. I wanted to be the complete work, not a shiny, eloquent presentation. Even though we have the same 24 hours in our day, how we manage that day matters. Do we make time to get enough rest, eat a well-balanced meal, take care of our temple, and then go out and balance our responsibilities? Or do we place the demands of life first day after day, then leave our vessel depleted of energy, focus, and fuel? How many times have you heard someone say, "I don't even have time to eat breakfast?" I'm not saying you must eat breakfast if that's not your thing. Some people don't. I don't always eat breakfast because I like intermittent fasting a lot, where I wait until a set time before eating anything. Yet, I'm still intentional about eating. I'm striving each day to drink my water so I stay hydrated and healthy. I believe in scheduling everything. I believe if it's not on the calendar, then it may not happen! You may not be a scheduler type of person, but you need to have some form of structure in your daily life. You should not just be "going with the wind" each day. Why? Life is constantly changing, moving, and going on. Without effectively managing your time, you can let an entire day go by without getting one thing done. There is one day a week that I allow for a "go with the flow" type of day. On this day, I sleep in a little later. I have what's called a "slow morning," where I ease my way into the day with no demands of work, the gym, my Google calendar, or answering phone calls and emails. This is the day I give myself grace to be Kamisha. Not the wife, the business owner, the interventionist, the mentor, or the friend. Just Kamisha. On this day, "I'm just a girl," so to speak. There are times I will plan things mentally that I aim to do, but they are not set in stone. For you, it may not be a day of the week that you have to "go with the flow," maybe an hour or two if your responsibilities are different from mine. I know my roles change with the seasons of my life. I previously had a very demanding office job where I was in the office from 7:00 am until 6:30 pm. The work-life balance was more difficult to manage. But even then, I didn't make excuses. I worked up some days and still went to the gym at 5:00 am, or I went right after work before going home. I ate light lunches to keep my energy level up and avoided heavy foods that would weigh me down. I did errands and business on my lunch break. Looking back, I realize that I made it happen for six years. Now that my work schedule is different, I have more ability to schedule things during different times. However, the time still has to be stewarded well. I'm going to share a few things that helped me steward my time well over the years. Being intentional is about making decisions. You have to choose that this is the lifestyle you want and lean into that. Come out of finding reasons that it can't work and push toward the solutions that can work.

Keys for effective time management that have been proven to work for me

1. Setting alarms in the morning
2. Structuring meal times (especially first meals of the day)
3. Using scheduling calendars for work, exercise, and appointments
4. Limiting social media for set times

5. Limiting phone conversations for set times (Not always answering your phone for unplanned conversations but finding out intentions of the call first)
6. Limiting tv time
7. Setting time to work out, walk, stretch, exercise
8. Scheduling time to connect with your spouse (setting dates for dinner, conversation, connecting if schedules are busy to avoid falling into "roommate mode")
9. Getting to bed at a time that gives you adequate sleep
10. Moving unplanned occurrences for planned unplanned appointments

These are all very effective keys I've used over the years that have given me results of time management. I've worked a demanding job and still wrote a book in less than a month. I've been able to mentor others while taking care of my household, working on fitness goals, and doing ministry assignments. This is not a brag, but I am just explaining that if I can do it, you can certainly do it. We are not different. I don't always want to get up right away when my alarm goes off in the morning, but I do. I don't always want to tell a friend that I only have 15 minutes to catch up and let's plan a date to have lunch, but I have had to. I don't always want to wait a day to watch a movie with my husband because we both have separate commitments planned for the night, but we have both learned to work well with this full lifestyle. If we can't wait for a full movie, we will watch a 30-minute comedy while catching up before we go to sleep or chat until the TV is watching us. Either way, there are things that we have to decide on to have effective time management. You can do it. I remember back in 2014, I was on a journey of learning my purpose and my gift of writing.

I took a leap of faith and started on my first book. "A Chosen Journey" at this time, I was new to all of this writing. That year, I did not watch TV all year. I had no interest in or time to devote to TV. I attended church three nights a week, served, worked a full-time job, and wrote my book. I didn't feel deprived of TV. I was focused on a greater outcome. Sometimes, you will have to forgo the average schedule and activities that most do if you want to get where most are not. Is it worth it to you for a life that exudes excellence?

She stewards her talents and gifts well.

Knowing your abilities is not enough; you must know how to steward those too. Serving is the best way to multiply what God gave you. He gives seed to the sower. The more you put out and give away, the more you will receive back. When you plant seeds, you will receive a harvest. There are many abilities that I had when I was younger that I've worked on over the years, and God has strengthened those gifts and talents. Have you heard of the phrase, "If you don't use it, you lose it?" That's true in itself. Have you ever heard someone sing so well at one point in their career, but then later on down the line, they get up to sing, and it doesn't sound the same anymore? Happens all the time. For different reasons, but that's just an example of how not using your voice often can cost you your voice. "Whatever your hand finds to do, do it with all your might." Ecclesiastes 9:10 It doesn't matter what your gifts or talents are, do them wholeheartedly.

Take care of them. Give them freely. At the same time, protect what you have. Guard those gifts and talents so that you can remain effective. All atmospheres and spaces aren't for you. All tables aren't for you to sit at, and all microphones don't need your voice speaking. Know how to be confident in what you have without the need for external validation, without needing to be "selected" by everyone. You are not supposed to be everyone's preferred choice. Not when you're peculiar and chosen. People will seek you out and find you and the right doors will open for you.

The right person will recommend you and tell others about you. You won't have to compromise or convince anyone to value you when you steward your gifts and talents well. Every church or event I've been invited to, every platform I've been on, has come most peculiarly, not by advertising myself as a speaker. I'm not shading or knocking anyone that does this. I'm just saying it never happened that way for me. I believe if I do everything with all my heart and mind, the right things will come to me. It's always been my story, and I like it that way. From the first book I wrote, I have always spoken these words throughout my life: "I will be a best-selling author one day." I believe that, without a doubt, will happen in my life. How it happens will not be for me to figure out, but I write every book with an excellent spirit. I take every word that I put to paper with heart. I don't write books to become a best-selling author. I wrote the books God told me to write and gave me the capacity and wisdom for. From that, he will cause me to be a best-selling author. He will go before me and cause it to happen in his timing and his way. Many different people have told me many times that my name will be known. I often think of this scripture: "I will make you into a great nation, and I will bless you; I will make your name great, and you will be a blessing. I will bless those that bless you, and whoever curses you I will curse, and all peoples on earth will be blessed through you." Genesis 12:2-3 This scripture is my foundation to never worry about seeking my greatness. I don't have to do anything extra; I only do the things I'm created and called to do with excellence. I don't have to step outside of my morals, values, and faith to get anything God has for me. You don't either. Sis, keep stewarding your gifts and talent well. Stay faithful to whatever it is you are supposed to do. Work on cultivating what God gave you, and in the right time and season, he will bring it to light. He will bless you; he will cause the light to shine on you. Even in your darkest moments, hard times, and challenges, keep using your gift. If your gift is to encourage others, keep doing it even when it seems like no one is listening or paying attention; if your gift is singing, keep singing, even if you have to cry sometimes behind the scenes due to the trials of life. If you are a teacher or a caregiver and you're gifted to steward children, keep being there and pouring into those children. They need you. You may be the only difference-maker in their life. No matter what it is, continue and steward well. "A man's gift makes room for him and brings him before great men." Proverbs 18:16: Let your gift make room for you. Many people have experienced life changes forever just by using their gifts and stewarding them well. Don't take what's in you lightly. Your gift and talent were created to make a difference.

She keeps the right people in her life.

We need an entire book for this part right here. An intentional woman doesn't take her connections casually. She knows the importance of having the right people in her life. She knows that the right people are necessary for her well-being. The right people in your life are such a gift and a blessing. Having people who help you in your hard times, encourage you through different seasons, and laugh with you in times of happiness and celebration is so good to have. Let's focus on this and get into it. We were not created on the earth to be alone. We were made to co-exist with others. We are supposed to have friends. The

Bible talks about friendship, the standard for it and how we should navigate friendship. "A friend loves at all times, and a brother is born for adversity." Friends should love you. They should be genuine and not have secret animosity, hidden agendas, or ulterior motives concerning you. They shouldn't be in it just for the benefit of being connected to you. They should also be there to help you when you need them. A good quality connection is mutual. This is not about being tit for tat (to retaliate or to give back as much as you receive), so there should be no score kept but mutual been both people have respect, love, and care for the other. The intentional woman does not repeatedly find herself in one-sided relationships or friendships where she is always pouring out, giving her last, showing up, giving support, and never getting anything back. No, sis, take a step back and observe. Remember I said previously that an intentional woman is a good listener? It comes into play here as well. Listen to what people are telling you in conversations. People are always telling and showing us how they feel about us. We are often too busy talking to hear the message. Over the years, I've learned so much about the proper connections. I had to be refined in this area a few times. In the past, when I was younger, I called everyone my friend. I used the term loosely, trusted easily, and gave freely. I had to go through a few things to learn what real friendship looked like. Now, I never resort to playing victim in any situation, so I won't go down the hole of telling about all my woes. I can say that I've experienced betrayal in friendship, jealousy, hurt, gossip, and ulterior motives in some shape or form. However, in those situations, I still look back and see the good times that were had. I see the moments where I may have overlooked some words, actions and conversations that led me to a place of disappointment, but I have zero regrets. I'm thankful for every situation. It has taught me to carry myself more intentionally. It has made me value my friendships on a deeper level because people don't have to be genuine, loving, and kind for real.

On the other hand, I've also experienced genuine, devoted, honoring, and pure-hearted friends. Everyone in my life currently that I give the title of friend is a real friend. They are so valuable to me. We are intentional about one another. My husband is my closest friend. I tell him everything, and I trust him with my feelings, hurts, concerns, and even desires. He has stewarded me well in that area. One thing I love about my husband is he isn't going to tell you anything about me I don't want to share. Doesn't matter who it is. Even his mother. He keeps the matters of my heart concealed. Now, I'm not holding everyone in my life to that same standard. But I'm glad that my husband has that standard and has proven it to me.

When it comes to our friends and colleagues, we have to know who we are connected to. If you know that someone is genuine, kind, and cares for you but doesn't keep confidence at a certain level, well, you have to handle that connection accordingly. Don't share your most intimate, private things with that person if they have shown they don't carry privacy in that same regard as you. While we are on the topic of privacy, you have to make sure that you are also stewarding people's information well in your connections. It doesn't matter if it's a business relationship, friend, colleague, mentee, or anyone who trusts you. You have a responsibility to steward that well. One thing I don't like to see personally is people who breach trust and confidentiality. It's an integrity thing for me. I've worked in spaces where confidentiality could cost you your job and even the law being broken. When working at a national bank, high-level intel, and even when working with children and families, privacy is key. So, I've always been one to keep certain information private. I can hear someone talking about someone and making an assumption, and I can know the actual details about it, but if it's not my place to say it, I will not say anything. I don't even want someone else to know that I know "the real truth" because that is not my place at that moment to reveal. We, as impactful women, operate with the utmost integrity and character when it comes to others. Again, have I always been so black-and-white about this? No. I haven't, but I'm thankful that the more intentional I became, the more I've stuck to these values and the more I have been entrusted with them. Keeping the right people around you means that everyone cannot be in your inner courts.

I watched an interview with the former first lady Michelle Obama, and she spoke on how she had to adjust her friendships when moving into the white house. She mentioned how there were some people she was friends with for 20-plus years that she remained close to, invited them to the white house, and continued closely interacting with them due to the posture of their relationship. She knew they could handle the friendship at the level she was now living on. She also said that there were some friends she kept but had to interact with from a distance because they were not able to fit in or understand her new lifestyle as a First Lady of the United States of America. She even briefly said how a few connections "fell off," meaning they did not remain at all due to the lack of depth or time of those connections. While I don't condone cancel culture or cutting people off for minute things, I do believe some people in your life will "fall off" on their own when you reach a certain altitude in life. Anyone who is not determined to grow with you is going to separate from you. It does not mean that they are bad people; it just means that they may not be aligned with the direction that you are going in. This is why we have to be intentional about the people God places in our lives. If you're like me, you may not have time to talk on the phone every day with your friends, meet up for dinner every week, or text back and forth daily. But, you may be able to check in on them to show up for an important occasion in their life. Send them a few dollars for a cup of coffee, comment on their latest post that you love them, schedule a time to chat on the phone, and the list goes on and on. If you want friends and good connections, you must show yourself to be

48

friendly and make the right effort. Don't be possessive, demanding, or offended if someone cannot communicate with you in the way that you desire to communicate with them. It could be for several reasons unknown to you. If you are feeling a change or a shift in a connection and you're unsure about it, the best thing to do is ask. If the person cares enough, they will offer you some explanation. If they do not feel the need to, they won't, and that will be your answer to knowing where you stand in their life.

As I said before, people are always showing and telling you how they feel about you. Believe them the first time. Never fight for a connection that is not mutual; never argue about something that is not helping you but hurting you. Even in times you are misunderstood and try to explain yourself and the person doesn't receive you, gracefully move on. Respectfully. You have a life to live, and in doing so, you will have to make uneasy decisions. However, it is your responsibility to help keep your heart pure and your eyes focused on good things. This leads me to my next point.

She sets boundaries

Having the right healthy boundaries in life as a woman will preserve your life, add years, take away stress and worry, and prevent so much turmoil. Do you enjoy a life of peace, tranquility, and ease? Then, you need to love having healthy boundaries. Often, when we hear the word boundaries, we may think that it pushes people away or makes us distant from others, but it really does the complete opposite. Having boundaries established in your life gives you the time, space, peace of mind, and energy to do all the necessary things that are needed in your life at that moment. Having boundaries protects your peace, your home, your children, and your relationships, and honors everything in the right way. Boundaries are simply limits or rules that define what is acceptable in a relationship or a situation. Everything thrives with limits and rules. Trust me. Having boundaries for your marriage can mean that you have time with yourself and your spouse when you turn your phones down, have a meal together, and go out on a night to keep the fire lit in your marriage. Dating my husband has been such a fun and fulfilling journey. We've never stopped dating since we met. Even when we have had challenging seasons, we found time to go out and connect. Those moments have helped us have a tough conversation, brought on laughter, or made us resolve a lingering issue. Setting boundaries on those nights made a difference in our ability to connect fully without any distractions. It's not just for marriage and relationships; boundaries are for life in general. An intentional woman is not afraid of holding fast to her boundaries. They don't have to be stated to everyone. You don't have to write a text or an email to tell everyone what your boundaries are. When the time comes to exercise them, that's when it matters most. People who have healthy boundaries are confident because it takes a level of confidence and security to implement boundaries. On the other hand, people who lack boundaries often deal with anxiety, low self-esteem, self-doubt, and resentment toward others. They feel obligated to be available for anyone at any time for any reason. They sometimes share too much personal information because they don't know how to honor their privacy. People don't know your boundaries, so they will sometimes say or do things that overstep your boundaries. When this happens, you don't have to get mad, get out of character, or tell them where to go. You have to exercise your boundaries and move on. I can think of plenty of times that my boundaries were crossed in the workplace, in my personal life, and relationships. I was called out of my name once in my former job position as I had to enforce a job policy on a customer. The customer had violated a contract, and I called her to come to the office so we could retrieve the asset. Instead of the customer accepting her fault and handling it cordially, she resorted to making a scene in the parking lot, being loud and boisterous, and challenging my position. I calmly told the lady, "Ma'am, you have the option of doing this the very easy way and handing me back the keys to the vehicle, or you can choose the hard way and have law enforcement come and retrieve the keys from you." I said nothing about her calling me out of my name, and that did not matter to me. I know who I am, so name-calling to me is the lowest form of an insult. Right after I calmly gave her the options at hand, she stopped yelling, threw the keys at me and proceeded to gather her things out of the car, still talking but much lower, and the premises. It was an easy fix. Now, as I reflected on this situation, had I gotten on the same level with this customer, yelling back at her, calling her names as she was calling me, and not remaining in my position, it could have gone another way. I could have lost my job, been seen as a crazy employee, or worse, law enforcement could have been called on both of us. Thankfully, that was never on my mind at that moment. I've never gotten the satisfaction of getting out of character with anyone. But boundaries were still exercised in that situation. No matter how difficult or simple the boundaries may be, they are needed in order to have a peaceful, healthy lifestyle. You don't want to operate through life as a doormat, a pushover, or a people pleaser. This is a whole different book in itself. People pleasing will rob you of your job your success, and alter your destiny. It can be passed down to your children as well when they grow up with a parent who does not show them how to enforce boundaries; they will never learn that for themselves. As a result, they will grow up attracting controlling, manipulative, and abusive relationships because they think it's normal. It's not normal, sis. For you or your children. Boundaries serve as protection in your life. T Everyone is not entitled to know how much money you make, how much your rent or mortgage is, when you plan on having children, why you haven't gotten married yet, what your credit score is, etc. The list can go on. You have to be okay with people not knowing everything about you. What do you have to prove? Sometimes, we even share things to try to make ourselves appear more "relatable" or "down to earth." You don't have to share anything personal that you don't want to share so that people will like you, accept you, or understand you. I used to find myself doing this years ago, trying to be so on a level with certain people who they wouldn't think I was stuck up or untouchable. In reality, it was those individuals who projected their personal feelings on me. When I began to connect with like-minded people, I realized that I had never come across as stuck up or untouchable. It was the confidence I carried that offended people with low confidence. It was the genuine personality that made the phony or deceitful individuals feel a certain way. Sometimes, in exercising your boundaries, you will often people. Especially people who don't have boundaries of their own. They will look at you like, "Who does she think she is?" Or feel entitled to know the details of your life. No one is entitled to anything in your life that you don't want to share. Sometimes, your privacy is the key to your peace. I've learned that the more you share or volunteer to give to others, the more they will make assumptions, predictions, or judgement about your life. You can tell

54

someone one thing about you that's so small, and they will use that small piece of importance to make an entire life story. This is why I'm very intentional now about my personal life and my boundaries. I'm not closed off; I'm not distrusting or skeptical. I'm discerning and discrete. There's a difference. I now know how to observe before sharing, how to listen before speaking, and how to make proper adjustments to my inner circle.

Here is a guide to having healthy boundaries

Rigid Boundaries	Porous Boundaries	Healthy Boundaries
Avoids intimate and close relationships	Overshares personal information	Values own opinions
Difficulty asking for help	Difficulty saying no to requests of	Doesn't compromise values for others
Keeps others at a distance to avoid rejection	Over-involved in other people's problems	Share personal information in an appropriate way
Very protective of personal information	Dependent on the opinions of others	Knows personal wants and needs and can communicate them
May seem detached from others	Accepting abuse and disrespect	Accepting when others say "no" to them and can say no without guilt

Rigid Boundaries	Porous Boundaries	Healthy Boundaries
Believes that no one is trustworthy	Fears rejection if they do not comply with others	Allows others in their lives and love freely
Uses hurt as a barrier	Uses guilt as a reason not to enforce boundaries	Treat each person appropriately when it comes to sharing
Lacks dependable relationships due	Tries to gain acceptance from everyone	Has a healthy, dependable relationships

She knows how to make declines and exits.

We often talk about receiving all the good things in life when we become an intentional woman, how the doors of opportunity will open for us, and how people in the right light will be drawn to us, but it's important to understand that this also means departures and exits are also unavoidable.

There will be times in your life when you have to say no. No more to certain situations that are not conducive to the woman you are becoming, no more to the things you allowed in the last season of your life, no more to being

56

improperly handled, and no more to selling yourself short in space that merely tolerated you but never full accepted or celebrated you. There were times in my life when I accepted things that I would never last one minute in now. My self-worth, my perception of my life, and my values have changed. They said it this way: "Yesterday's price is not today's price." It costs to access you. Your time, love, and energy are not for sale, but they cost you something. It cost me so much to live this life of peace, freedom, and joy. It cost me friendships that were no longer right for me; it cost me opportunities that I could have taken but would have compromised my integrity or values; it cost me walking away from money that would have been a headache to accept in the long run. It cost me status and acceptance with people, but it granted me favor with God for sticking to my values and always striving to do what is right. Either way, it costs you something.

How do we know when it's right to decline or exit as an intentional woman? When the cost is greater than the gain. Simple. You have to make the right judgement on the situations in your life. Is the friendship worth working through the disagreements, the misunderstandings, and the hard conversations? Yes, if it is a great benefit to your life, then the challenges your two are currently facing. Is the job worth staying at for the time being in order to get your finances in order? Yes, if you are able to go to work every day knowing that you are there for a reason and a purpose, but no, it's not worth it if you are leaving work sitting outside your house in tears due to the stress, anxiety, and weight the job is placing on you. Is it worth serving in this organization even though you may have to deal with some opposing views and a few difficult personalities and put in more effort than the rest? Yes, if you can see the light at the end of the tunnel and know that you are doing it for a bigger reason than yourself. However, if helping that organization is causing you to feel anxious, stressed, and worried and robbing you of your daily peace, then it may be time to exit gracefully.

How to intentionally and gracefully exit

Sis, this is different for everyone, but what I can tell you is that how you exit is how you will enter the next phase, how you will walk through the next door. So do it with intention and do it gracefully. I've resigned from jobs, turned down invitations, and ended relationships, and each time, it was done differently. I remember when I was in my 20s, and I resigned from a fast food job I had been working at for about 4 years. The job was so good because I made decent money and I had an amazing manager. I still have her number to this day. She really was one of the first managers to teach me about commitment and dedication. Before her, I'd only had one job, and I was not dedicated to that job in any way. It was just there for my weekly paycheck at the young age of 16 years old. By the time I worked for this next manager, I was around 18, and I was there until I was about 21. When I finally decided to resign, after working another job and keeping this one as a fill-in, I decided to write my manager a nice typed letter with my written signature. When I handed it to her, it was hard for me to do. I had seen many people come and go, walk off, quit, and even take breaks without coming back. So the last thing I wanted was for her to see me as leaving her hanging. At 21, these were my thoughts. As I stood there, she silently read the letter, and she looked at me without speaking. I was expecting her to tell me off or say something harsh. She said, "This is the most professional and sweetest letter I've ever received, and I'm so proud of you. I'm really going to miss you,

59

Kamisha." As I type this now, the emotions return to my 21-year-old self. Watching her turn pink and wipe her eyes, I, too, started holding back my tears. It was a moment I won't forget because I never imagined a resignation to go that way.

Even though we both knew it was time for me to move on with my life, I graduated from undergrad and received my Bachelor's degree; we still spent 4 years together on a weekly basis. She watched me grow and go through challenges, triumphs, friendships, and work situations. She had been like a work mentor to me. Telling me about my attitude when I would tell her I wasn't coming in on holiday and telling me that I had to learn how to be flexible. Lol. We would go at it sometimes, but at the end of the day, I really respected and appreciated her, and I saw how much she appreciated me. Ashley, if you ever read this, thanks for everything. Knowing when to exit a season of your life gracefully is the key to walking toward your destiny. Growth requires change, change requires new things, and new things require us to leave the old things behind. "Behold, I am doing a new thing: now it springs forth, do you not perceive it? I will make a way in the wilderness and rivers in the desert." Isaiah 43:19

When a new thing is happening, you have to see it. Don't be stuck in your old ways, in the old season, in your comfortable place; you can't walk into the new place. As uncomfortable and uncertain as it may seem, God will make a way. Walking away from that relationship that wasn't good for you and caused you years of pain will be hard, but God will make a way. He will heal your heart and bring you out on the other side.

Any time you have to decline or make an exit, be gracious. Remember, the same people you see going up, you may see them again. Make sure that anything in your control is done right. It's not up to you how the other person receives the decline or the exit, but it's up to you how you deliver it. Never be mean, haughty, or disrespectful to someone. No matter how bad you feel like you were treated, how much you were ready to leave that job, how that friend slandered you behind your back. Do unto others as you would want them to do toward you. I promise you this will always keep you in a posture to be blessed.

Think of it this way: if the person is exiting your life or you are walking away, what's the need to be angry or upset now? Sure, it may have hurt you and still could be hurtful, but remain sober respectful, and make sure you are setting up your future for peace and prosperity. We reap what we sow to others, so be intentional about how you decline or leave a situation. If someone invites you to be a part of something that does not align with you, don't be rude or make unneeded or hurtful comments as to why you can't take part. Thank them for thinking of you, but politely decline the opportunity at this time. You don't have to lie, make up a reason why you can't, say you're going to be doing something else, politely decline and move on. This makes you a woman of class, dignity, and respect. People will respect you more even when you decline to help or do something for them, but you keep it respectful and honest. I've had people tell me that they respect my decision for not partaking in certain things, not going to certain places, and not agreeing on certain topics, but it didn't negatively affect the connection. It's not what you say but how you say it; it's not what you do all the time but how it's done. Represent yourself well, and it will always pay off in the long run. Everyone will not always like it when you decline or exit a situation, but that's not your responsibility. It's your responsibility to be a good representation of yourself and treat people well in the process. That is how you can be trusted with more in life, by being a good steward over others through the good, bad, and hard times. You will be able to influence people in your world and also to do the right things.

Chapter 5

She sees possibilities more than problems

Your perspective and ability to see through the eyes of faith and possibility are going to change the trajectory of your life. Intentional woman, there will be challenges, obstacles, problems, and setbacks in your life. That is a part of life's experience. We cannot control everything that happens to us, but we can always control how we chose to see and believe. There are always possibilities that lie in every hard time, challenging situation, and even what you would call a "bad day." The woman who can look past the inevitable and focus on the possible is unstoppable. This is a woman who is not led by her fleeting emotions. This woman can stand tall in the face of adversity and see what's around the corner: a win. A better day after a hard one. She can see herself smiling beyond the tears that she is crying. She can see hope in the midst of a loss. Sis, what do you see in your life right now? What are your exceptions for the remainder of this year? What is your focus on? The intentional woman is able to set her hope on things above;

she is able to look at her future with joy and wonder. "She is clothed with dignity and strength, and she laughs without fear of the future." Proverbs 31:25

She refuses to worry.

Worrying is putting a negative down payment on something that may never even happen. It's obsessing over something that may have already happened and placed you in a place of disarray. Don't allow anything in your life to cause worry because it drains so much of your joy and peace to be in this state of mind. I've been given some negative news before. Yet I had to make a choice. I'm either going to handle the part of this that I handle and walk in peace, or I'm going to give away my peace to worry and fear. I refuse to let anything or anyone have access to my peace. Therefore, worrying cannot be my portion in life. When I feel myself faced with worry, I immediately go into prayer and cast that care to God. Why? Simply because he told me to. "Casting the whole of your care (all your anxieties, all your worries, and all your concerns, once and for all) on Him, for He cares about you (with deepest affection, and watches over you very carefully) 1 Peter 5:7

When someone may hurt you or treat you in a way you don't expect or deserve? What's your first reaction? To hurt them back? I hope not. That's a life of a never-ending cycle of dysfunction. Hit me, I hit you. You'll be going through life trying to even the score with everyone. I would not recommend it. Or, when someone mishandles you, you can choose to seek an understanding of why they did it. Everything has its purpose. Even the unfortunate events. Sometimes, it's not even personal; sometimes, it has everything to do with them. It could be something internal they are dealing with. It could be an unresolved space they are living in with themselves. It could be a bad day. It could really be anything. We can't allow anyone's posture to change us and keep us from our purpose. This is why I choose to see the best, no matter how bad a situation may seem. For years, I was told by people around me, "You're always giving people the benefit of the doubt." Or "You're too nice to people that aren't nice to you." I used to hear this and take this as a negative. Or I'd say that people took my kindness for weakness. Now that I understand the call on my life, I don't run from the fact. I do give people a lot of grace. I do see the best in the worst of situations and sometimes the worst kind of people. It's not weakness, it's strength. It's not a disadvantage; it's a blessing to me that I have that kind of sight. While I've learned how to accept people for who they are and adjust accordingly. I'll never have a desire to hate a person. That's not who I am or who I was designed to be.

Hate is too expensive. Hate leads to bitterness, and that leads to sickness, mental illness, physical illness and even death. Trust me; many illnesses are caused by the disrupted nervous and immune systems, which the matters of the heart and mind can cause. You want to have your heart and mind clear at all times. This is what helps you to walk in limitless possibilities. You can move with ease, peace, love, and freedom. Your countenance will be pleasant and joyful. You will glow when you live this way. "A merry heart makes a cheerful countenance." Proverbs 15:13

She limits her complaints.

There are so many times that you will be tempted to vent, complain, or express things in your life that may be frustrating, bothering you, or not going right. This is natural. When someone at a restaurant gives us terrible service, doesn't make our food correctly, or doesn't treat us with the right hospitality, it may be natural to share this with someone close to you in conversation. This is a natural part of sharing with others. Yet, as an intentional woman who understands her impact, you should limit your habits of complaining. Use your words and your influence effectively. There was an actual time when my husband and I traveled to a city away from home to try a restaurant we heard about.

We had a very unpleasant experience. The food was not prepared correctly, the wait was long despite us making a previous reservation, and the server's effort was not aimed at providing excellent service. I am a person who has worked in restaurants, so I see an experience at a restaurant from all angles. I can tell if a place is busy and understaffed, so I show grace. I can tell if a server is overwhelmed with too many tables in an area, and I can tell if there is a disconnect between the order being taken and the cook. I also don't always believe that the customer is always right. I've been on the end of the spectrum where customers were downright wrong, rude, and loud. When my husband and I experienced this unfortunate experience. We did not cause a scene; we didn't treat the server the way she treated us (kind of condescending toward us). We paid the bill, left her a tip still, and left on the long ride home. I went on Google and left the restaurant an honest, detailed review of where our experience did not meet our expectations. I was very matter-of-fact in the review; I was not rude, not emotional, but honest. A few days later, I received an email from the restaurant manager asking if she could give me a call. I accepted that invitation. While on the phone, the manager immediately apologized for the experience we had, explained some things that took place and asked us if we would consider returning for a better experience. I talked this over with my husband. In reality, we didn't need a free meal. But, because of the sincerity of the manager and her desire to see us again, we chose to schedule another time to visit. This time, the manager greeted us at the door, took our order, and talked with us. We had a much nicer experience. I believe there are times when we should know how to express our complaints or even know when it's not necessary. There have been several other times that I have had negative experiences at different places, but I felt no need to leave a review or say anything to the staff. But I gratefully made the best of it and moved on.

If there are times you want to express yourself, state your concerns, or address issues, I believe it is important to do so. There's a big difference between being a woman who isn't afraid to address necessary issues and being a complaining woman. No one likes to really spend much time with a complainer. Complaints made too often will dilute what you have to say and lessen your impact. Can you recall a time you may have been scrolling online and you saw a person making a negative post? The first time, it may have captured your attention. It is a statistical fact that people pay more attention to negative posts than positive ones. This is why when a person posts something like "Today was a good day," it gets very little traction. People see it and continue scrolling. This is not to say that people think badly of the post; it's just nothing that many people care to respond to. However, when you see someone online venting about a breakup, speaking about a poor experience, or saying something like, "I can't believe such and such happened to me today, worst day ever." Those types of statements are full of comments, remarks, questions, and add-ons of their opinions. As an intentional woman, you don't want to draw much of this type of attention. This speaking, venting, and complaining will always get you looked at, heard, and seen, but it may not be what you want to be known for in the long run; when you are known as a complainer, it's a detractor. Others may avoid doing business with you, partnering or sharing something with you because you display more complaints than positivity. When it comes to social media, sometimes you have to delete the whole post before hitting "post."

Ask yourself, "Is this helpful to the reader?" "Is this necessary to share right now, or am I seeking some sort of validation of my current feelings?" Again, I'm not telling you to mute yourself or become self-conscious of what you want to say. I'm just suggesting that you be mindful of the impact you can be making. Even offline, there are times you want to choose your complaints wisely. I strive not to complain to my husband as a wife. I want to always express my concerns, suggestions, or issues in a very impactful way. Everything doesn't need to be addressed at all times. If I leave the house for work in the morning, that is not the time for me to bring up an issue with my husband when we have no time to discuss, reason, or resolve it. I don't feel it appropriate to file a complaint against him and leave. I sometimes will wait until later in the day when we are relaxing, home from work, watching something on TV, sitting close, bonding, and having a good time. Then, I may bring up what I need to say in a way that doesn't destroy the mood. My husband will likely receive it better. Lady, you have to know how to read the room and use wisdom and discernment at the right time to express yourself. I've had to learn this over the years, and I'm glad I've become much more refined in my communication, the timing of my words, and my delivery. Even in the workplace, use your words, your suggestions, and complaints with care. The type of field of my career is very reliant on relationships and building good communication. As an interventionist, I speak the most with parents, therapists, healthcare professionals, and children. There is a lot of interaction on a daily basis, and effective communication is key. I experience many situations where I could offer up complaints, critiques, and corrections to individuals, but I may find it an intentional point to let my voice be more helpful, encouraging, and insightful than complaining and critical. A therapist may take a while to get back to me in an email.

Sometimes, it's days longer than it should take. While I could respond with, "Hello, I sent this email two days ago. Can you respond to my inquiry?" I may say, "Good morning. I am just following up on the previous email. I know you may have received many by now, and I just wanted to make sure this didn't slip through the cracks. Look forward to hearing from you soon!" Almost every single time, I get a very gracious, accountable, positive response. I didn't aim to complain about how long it took to get a response; my main goal was to get my inquiry taken care of. That's the ticket: focusing on the solution at hand, not the problem. Making the possibilities the focus and not the problem is such a game changer. People will really respect you and value your input when you limit your complaints and make your words count.

She sees the best in others.

Your ability to still see the best in others will really be one of the best gifts you can have for yourself. There will be people in your life who may treat you less than you deserve; they will unintentionally or purposely hurt you. They will sometimes overlook you, come against you, reject you, or take your kindness as their opportunity to misuse you. Still, you must keep your heart pure toward others; that way, your vision can be blessed. Listen, I used to get mad with myself in the past for always trying to see the best in another person even after something hurtful happened to me by that same person. Now, with time, experience, and wisdom, I am thankful for that ability. It doesn't mean that you have to accept unacceptable treatment, behaviors, repeat offenses, and allow people in the same space with you. It means that you are willing to show grace, compassion, and forgiveness and move forward to see the best in the person. Even if you decide that you will move on from a job, a relationship, end a friendship, whatever capacity it may be. It's so good when you can think back on the experience or speak about the season of your life without bitterness, resentment, and anger. Trust me, I've dealt with situations that, at the moment, I felt were not forgivable. But, as a mature, intentional, God-centered woman, I have chosen to forgive those who hurt me, love my enemies, and do good to them that may do the opposite to me. This has been my gift from God. This has granted me peace in my life that surpasses anything I can truly understand. This allows me to walk into a room without having to hang my head down or without anxiety rising in me around a certain person; this allows me to keep a smile on my face, no matter who has erased it or brought me to tears. I know now that every single thing in my life will work out for my good if I keep my heart and mind pure toward people. This is the same for you. There is nothing that anyone can do to you that can steal your vision, your pure heart, and your mind. Unless you chose to give it away. So what if they lied to you, cheated you in business, broke you in a vulnerable season, and never let anyone's poison keep you from your purpose? If I can be honest, some things happened in our lives to show us how to operate better, to show us how to have compassion for others in that same situation. Sometimes, we have to feel a sting in life because we never understand how it feels to be in a certain position until it happens to us. You have to make a choice. It won't always feel like a time to think the best of someone, but it is never a bad idea to do so. Every place of employment I've ever had; when I look back, all I can really remember the most is the good times I had at that job, the lessons I learned, the skill sets I was taught, and the close relationships I formed that helped me in those seasons. Yes, I have some memories of the challenges and the hard situations I had to overcome, but those memories are few and far between. Why? Because I don't choose to allow negative memories to outweigh the good ones. Let me share something with you. About 10 years ago, I was living in Charleston, South Carolina, where I spent most of my teen, college, and young adult years. I was working at a very well-known bank at the time. I was commuting about 35 minutes one way to work on a good day if there were no accidents on the interstate. I would clock in the bank at 8:00 am, and we would open at 9:00 am. I'd leave for the day around 5:30 pm or sometimes 6:00 pm and go right to my second job. From around 6:00 pm to 10:00 pm. I had a full day during this time of my life. My bank manager at the time was a woman who was very organized and proactive and believed in getting a job done at any cost. She came up with this unwritten idea for the bank tellers to come to work at 6:30 am on Monday mornings so we could count all the overnight, weekend business deposits that we dropped over the weekend. She wanted us to get a head start on the Monday rush. We all complained about this, "Why don't we just do these bags when we come in a regular time on Monday?" That is what many of us asked. Our complaints didn't change the outcome. We were coming in on Monday morning. For a while, I resented this manager with a passion; getting up two hours earlier on a Monday put such a sour taste in my mouth. The only benefit I could see to this is that I got to work faster due to beating all the interstate traffic. Still, my close coworker and I would complain so badly each Monday. Mumbling and grumbling to ourselves as we counted up all these deposit bags. However, after a month or so of doing this on Mondays, the complaining grew less. We got adjusted to the schedule, and it became a normal thing for us until, I don't remember the point. Now, ten years later, I'm still connected to this former supervisor. I realized that she did things to bring out the best in us as a team. Even though, at the time, it seemed so extra, so hard, and I didn't really like her so much during that season. I learned that she was a great person who saw the good in me and that she helped bring it out. Even after leaving that job, we stayed connected. She invited me to personal celebrations in her life, and I even hired her to speak at an event I hosted. I shared that small part of my life as a teller, and I have such fond memories of working at that bank. The co-workers, the day-to-day work, and all the hard lessons I learn are core memories of my young adult career. I wouldn't be where I am as a business owner, a mentor, and an author had I not experienced those times in my life. Sis, I am challenging you right now to make an intentional choice to see the good in where you are today. Right here and now. It may be rough and may not feel like it's working out in your favor, but trust me, something is happening for you. Things are working out for your good. Keep your mind and heart in a place of gratitude, and I promise you will reap the blessings.

Chapter 6

She aims to impact, not impress

To impress, by definition, means to influence someone's opinion or feelings, to cause someone to feel admiration or interest, or to fix something firmly in someone's memory or mind. Words associated with impress are sway, persuade, inspire, touch, or affect.

When you walk into an interview and meet someone for the first time, the first impression will indeed matter, especially in a situation where you may not see the individual again.

In cases where the time is limited, and the relationship is brief, you may feel the need to make a great first impression. I know when I go to a restaurant for the first time, that first encounter will make a big impression on whether or not I return. There are times that impression will be applicable in your life. However, making an impact will go so much further. We live in a world where people spend thousands of dollars on appearances, gadgets, and belongings, all in an effort to impress other people around us. Very few people really take the time to make an impact on the lives of others. Many times, it's all about "looking the part" or appearing to be successful. I will say there is nothing wrong with looking excellent and appearing nice in your own right. Those are great qualities to have. It's just important that we don't allow superficial things to weigh more than the aspects of us that will make an impact. Would you rather someone only remember you by how you looked, what you wore, the car you drive? Or, would you rather be remembered in your life by the lives that you touched with your words or your actions, how you taught someone something they didn't previously know? How did you step in and help someone win in an area of their life that they were struggling with? Intentional woman, you have the power to make a lasting impact. Seek that first above the impressions. I love rooting for what society calls "the underdog." This is characterised as a person who "seems" least likely to succeed or win. Those individuals are often overlooked, rejected, underestimated, and not favored by people initially. In a game, the underdog is the team that may not have won the most games, but they have a solid team on board with great potential. When this kind of person achieves things that others never thought they could, it leaves a lasting impact on the minds of others. It shows people that you can't always judge a book by its cover. It proves that the loudest is not always the smartest in the room. It also shows that talk is cheap and that actions are what cashes out the most. A person of impact will transform a situation, and they will leave lasting memories or change. They will alter or modify systems, ideas, and the way something is done for the better. One of the greatest assignments I have been given is being a mentor. This is not a role I was ever trying to get into myself, but rather, it was given to me by God, I believe. Back in 2019, a younger girl at my church asked me if I would be her mentor. Not really knowing what that meant, I said, "Sure!" A week later, another young girl asked me, and then her sister and another. In a month or so, I had about six girls who had separately asked me if I would be their mentor. Shortly after speaking with my Pastor about this, I began mentoring at my local church. Never considered having a nonprofit organization, which would come 5 years later. I gave what I had to create a positive impact in the lives of those girls. We didn't have any money for funding, flashy things, logos, or trips. We had group classes; we spent time sharing, learning, and talking about things that would help them in the years to come. I never wanted the girls I mentored to be impressed with me as a person. After all, I am not the type of leader to draw extra attention to my life because I'm a flawed person who God graces to have the knowledge and wisdom that I have. Nothing really so amazing about me, just what God has given me to give back to others. In these very simple yet interesting years, the girls were able to find more confidence, learn that their voice mattered, build other relationships with girls their age, and get out of some of the shyness that many of them had. We would do activities where they had to share before the small group. For them, at first, it was intimidating, but over time, I saw them blossom, grow, and change into beautiful, intelligent, God-fearing young women. Some have graduated high school, some are attending college, others have started their own business, and so many aspects. One day, I asked the girls to write down why they were continuing to be mentored and what they got out of the program. One of the mentees said, "I've developed a strong mind since you mentored me." I did so much to hold back my tears in front of that person.

That let me know that an impact was made. Impacting another person is not about how they admire you all the time, how good you appear to be, or how they want to even be like you. It's how you can influence the person to grow or change for the better. It's planting a seed in someone's life that may not blossom right away like my previous supervisor did for me. I couldn't see the value in her right then and there, but over time, I realized how special she was to that time in my life. I am to make an impact anyplace I'm given the chance. It's not hard to do. It just requires you to be yourself and be mindful of your words and actions. They have an impact, whether positive or negative. I'm going to list just a few ways that you can become impactful, and I'm sure you will see that you are already doing some of these things, but maybe you never knew how much they really mattered. They matter a lot, and your impact is greater than you know.

1. Be authentic- Don't try to move or operate like someone else just because you see something working for them. Do what is genuine for you. Speak like your authentic self, and show up as the real you.

2. Be consistent- People will watch what you do twice as much as they listen to your words. You always want to make sure that your actions are lining up with what you speak.

3. Be kind- No matter what the situation is, even if it is during a conflict or negative situation, don't lose your kindness or respect. People will remember how you handled the situation.

4. Be gracious- This is a form of humility. People will make mistakes and not always do things right toward you; you haven't always been done right by others. Showing grace makes an impact.

5. Be giving- Give what has been freely given to you without thinking you're going to be at a loss. If you have information that can help someone, help them. It's so much better to give than receive. You may think what you have to offer doesn't matter, but you never know, so don't hold back.

6. Be a leader- don't wait around to see what others will do in every situation. Learn to lead, take action, and be the first example if you know that you are able to. Sometimes, it just takes one person to do it, and then others will follow.

7. Make strong connections- You don't have to be popular or know every single person to have strong quality connections that impact. Be willing to be a part of a community or cause greater than yourself. Serve, volunteer, support a business, attend a family gathering, host something with friends to bring people together.

8. Cultivate self-awareness- Learn to listen without interrupting, criticizing, belittling, or being forceful in interactions; strive to listen more than speak so that when you speak, it will be more effective. Learn the details about a person or a situation before making an assumption. Ask questions, and come to an educated conclusion based on facts rather than feelings or misinformation.

9. Work on yourself constantly- If you are always finding ways to improve, you will always be an impactful person. A wise person knows they never stop growing while they are living. They are finding ways to improve, learn, and share their processes. This kind of person refrains from being judgmental because they know that they, too, were not always where they are and also are aware that they have more work to accomplish.

As you continue throughout your journey and you implement these tools, you will be so intentional with your life that you won't go through it, living by default, settling for less, and just taking what's handed to you. No, you will go out and create the life that you desire to live through your faith, your words, and your actions all together. They all go hand in hand. Faith without works is dead. You also can be running a race in life that is going nowhere fast because you aren't pairing that labor with strong beliefs, faith, and a good heart and mind. We don't want our work to be without a cause or in vain. We want everything we do as young women, working women, single women, married women, mothers, aunts, and grandmothers, to be effective and impactful. Sometimes, this means leaving behind that instant gratification, the need to be accepted and validated by everyone, and the need to save everyone when we can only really change ourselves. Sometimes, it's giving up that control that we are seeking to have and allowing God to do his greatest work in us and through us. That also means resting. Sis, as you read the close of this book, my hope and desire for you is that this unlocks a new level of your journey as a woman. You rest in knowing that you have power and purpose, that you believe that your voice carries, and so do your words and actions. You realize in the midst of all of your roles, responsibilities, and hats that you are free just to be. Every day of your life does not have to be on a tight, unyielding schedule in order to be intentional. Some days, you will intentionally turn off the phone, TV, and all the devices, and just be you. Even then, you are still successful, still worthy of good things, and still loved. I want you to realize that even on your lowest-performing day, you are doing a great job in life. Your worth isn't measured by your money, your education, marking off your "to-do" list or anything of those changeable factors. You are simply a woman chosen to live out her life with purpose, passion, and power. You have only scratched the surface. May the days fill you with joy, peace, and more understanding of your life assignment. May you walk into rooms like you were sent there, and may you hold your head up with the quiet confidence you need to navigate this season and beyond? Let me remind you of this: you are exactly who and where you need to be.

Made in the USA
Middletown, DE
10 May 2025